ECCOLO

Hal Coase was born in Surrey and grew up in the Black Country. His poetry has been published by Carcanet in *New Poetries VII* (2020) and Prototype in *Prototype 5* (2023). In 2018, he was shortlisted for the White Review Poet's Prize. In 2024, he received the Harper-Wood Studentship from St John's College, Cambridge. He lives in Rome.

ECCOLO
POEMS

Hal Coase

CARCANET POETRY

First published in Great Britain in 2025 by
Carcanet
Main Library, The University of Manchester
Oxford Road, Manchester, M13 9PP
www.carcanet.co.uk

Text copyright © Hal Coase 2025

The right of Hal Coase be identified as the author
of this work has been asserted in accordance with the
Copyright, Design and Patents Act of 1988; all rights reserved.
No part of this book may be used or reproduced in any manner for
the purpose of training artificial intelligence technologies or systems.

A CIP catalogue record for this book is
available from the British Library.

ISBN 978 1 80017 495 5

Book design by Andrew Latimer, Carcanet
Typesetting by LiteBook Prepress Services
Printed in Great Britain by SRP Ltd, Exeter, Devon

The publisher acknowledges financial
assistance from Arts Council England.

For my sister

CONTENTS

2nd January — 9

I

Animal Alphabets — 13
Pray'r — 37

II

Lyric — 41
Schadograph — 42
The Meantime — 43
Rodeo Pleat — 46
Gulfs — 48
Translating Sandro Penna — 51
The Cheese and the Worms — 52
February — 53
The Moderns — 54
The Move — 57
Crib — 58
Portrait of the Artist Soutine by His Beef Écorché — 59
Thetic — 63
Ducts — 64
Anatomia — 66
Fragment: Berlin 3024 — 67

III

Ochre Pitch — 71

Paraphrase — 93

Acknowledgements — 95

2ND JANUARY

> *Reading by the candle of life*
> *we complete his ledgers*
>   John Berger

It was just evening
on a coastal path
in the country where
you found a home
to live through.
The view was what
you'd notice in it:
vines, roots, dirt,
stories – touchable
and tended to.

I could have met
you at the turn,
talking of love
with a labourer.
I would have known
you, secretary, by
that 'I don't know
but I imagine so.'
Your doubts held
hope like January.

You might have
stopped to voice
the soil's unheard
work, draw its
fruits beneath
a borderless blue

and listen as if life
depended on it
(far oftener than not,
it does, you knew).

I

ANIMAL ALPHABETS

*We do not need more data,
but more mind.*
George Santayana

o

Al – for better
days, I've bought
you a book
      that can be read

only after
you've learnt
what can't
      be said.

I

Bent swift,
like speech,
the otter
  lands in water.

No words
can reach
a body's
  candid awe.

2

We fed the snout,
and growing quiet
its waxy lips
      took life in hand.

Where's the mouth?
So starts our quest
to understand
      on all six legs.

3

Most all delights
are dolphin-like –
in but leaping
      barely known.

Bright thing, listen:
let's age again
and heedlessly
      mislay the nouns.

4

I mislabel
the old branch.
It is a marled stag
      with cross.

Overhead: a happiness.
This sun parcels
out ten steps
      to the rocks.

5

At the deep end
of a field:
this rabbit
      blows a kiss.

Low in the den,
her cautioned life
snugs a deft
      ear to russet.

6

No, patience
isn't enough
to save us all,
        but entrance

to vegetable sense:
low and rough,
an old canticle
        to greenéd must.

7

I was a boy
laid sudden
as a starlet
      gone to ground.

It is a joy
to be hidden,
disaster not
      to be found.

8

A language
doesn't grow,
but is equal
         of its habitat:

a land's age,
the hedgerow,
a lark's calling
         tit-for-tat.

9

And what did	E che cosa
you want?	volevi?
To call up my	Chiamare i miei
beloveds,	amati,
to feel the air	sentire l'aria
belaboured	elaborata
on the earth	sulla terra
beloved.	amata.

10

Like, for example:
Holofernes –
with his heed
      unto hir toun

she wente,
with his head
exampled
      as her truth.

11

Vampire Lyric,
you've howled at
every door
       but mine.

Now wick of
song, go down
for the good
       of rhyme.

12

Ished astray,
slow snow
falling like
      governance

on angerland.
White glow,
black blaze of
      kingfisher days.

13

*If difference,
then resistance.*

A poem
    like measure

of both:
closing
and disclosing
    distance.

14

Of paramount
importance:
that smile
     when you

fumble a sound,
then glance
down. Why?
     If I knew

15

The force
of her laughter
barrels through
      the day.

Carry your
hereafters,
squirrel them
      away.

16

There is no place
without its Persephone.
Even the heath,
    brackened, sewn

shut by April's
fussiness
has a streak
    of elsewhere.

17

Campfire mimicry
of colza and corn.
I can't believe
    it will end

in frostiness.
Your warmth
on me relieves
    a winter.

18

Kingdom,
we're coming,
pleached trees
 beware.

We're crafting
a home
out of branches
 and air.

19

Loiter in
the summer,
become a
    worrier,

your voice
is wrung
and strained
    by this.

20

The heron
swaggered
on Ponte Rotto,
      today.

From here on
in, the bridge
is your
      bouquet.

21

Your philosopher
says we've lost,
and having
    lost

we are lost
where we are.
Ei.   We must
    not lose

2 2

We sift
the wild
alphabets,
      and then

we rest
godishly
in a tight
      spot.

PRAY'R

Sant'Ayana
of the valley
strong flower

breathe in
breathe out
enrapture me

II

LYRIC

o major I
o major me
o major time
in a minor key

SCHADOGRAPH

over out of season artichokes
he tells me time doesn't exist

we muddle through the bill
and walk a high-walled road

that cuts a park in two
south towards the river

the way the roots go down
easing with need

to the plain apartment
where he still lives

THE MEANTIME

In this poem, I tell you how the frost came.
For days we had been waiting to park,
we set up watch in the blue play

of the city's syntax, black tea in a flask,
the damp of our breath panning out,
our talk low like the wall of an orchard.

I'd lost how to plot without air-quotes
and you'd reply with a run-up that went past
itself, then the illiterate quiet of hope,

food, and sleep. The last decade
seemed all method, the line and form
of a spreadsheet or some shrinking lake

with its fingerbones of toasted iron.
In your language and mine, silence
is not sharp, and suffers no harm:

a patient art that is like the best of us
allotted. In the glove compartment,
I found 64 well-thumbed signs of life –

>   receipts
>   change
>   fiver
>   vaseline
>   torch
>   toffees
>   tennis ball
>   cap

                poppers
                red pencil
                map
                hammer
                fortune fish
                mask
                crisp packets
                keys
                condoms
                papers
                guide
                lighter
                tram ticket
                fine
                sunglasses
                glove
                three photographs
                silver
                gold
                mercies

You slept curled on the backseat. I loved
your barefoot insistence that spring
is dreamt from the warmth of mud.

On the radio was everyman pretending
they are more than capable of being judged,
and on your birthday, suddenly, a bulletin

from a country that has had enough.
You woke up, we spoke about light pollution,
Pasolini's fireflies, the emptiness of force.

You said, roughly: a good photo guards
the iris – a thorn to petals. I did not 'agree'
but the sun, in that moment, came hard

from elsewhere. It had been rummaging,
it was weighty with all the stolen clarity of glass
and water, which it lapped now on the streets.

I cracked the door, met the cold with a gasp
and leapt out here where I had failed
even as I knew – and then the frost had come.

RODEO PLEAT

Morning. You asked if
we had stayed all night
together, sitting, would
it — the day — have differed?

Why do I remember it so?
Because you've asked me.
So, I remember, completely,
that morning with him.

I remember:
I asked straight
out if I could
keep his clothes.

My voice: can I keep
your clothes?
And his voice (thin,
rested, going places):

keep them, put them on,
wear them out.
Out and down to town?
Or out and down to nothing but threads?

And, y'know, once, he had,
before, crossed
the river on horseback
but not in these clothes

(these yarns fit shapely
after a winter's slimming)
and once, he had,
after crossing, made

a masterpiece of not
listening to kindly people
who left tired and smitten.
Is it possible that this

is the first skin I'll cut
him out of and next
century – another place?
In his clothes with a gap

between my leg and the cut
of the leg, I feel myself
coming to and memory
starts to feel like
tomorrow's business.

GULFS

There is no falling
that says more than
its weight. Measure
corresponds. So falling

falling shows the man
to be the falling,
to be that fall —
sured aim

of what is let fall
like a song that
with ease runs
the length of day.

He was a hard fall.
It took three cities
to fall further,
farther than his all.

    *

OK. Paradise:
the shift of every
thing of paradise
to paradise.

— your nails,
the word 'up', or
accents you put on
when hungry,

these increments
of elsewhere,
the same in all
but who it touches,

the nameless
sounds we trade
in a life's
hiatuses.

    *

*San Luigi,
Rome.*
Say, the light
crossed

by its own
strength,
the bracket
of a man

who hitches
up
the alley's
curtain

to see
the faces:
coins
for counting.

    *

It comes of age
at the end
of history,
you almost taste

the iron
of progress
that fastens
the pane.

No wonder then
that we prefer
how words
collide

and sever
their parts
into fair
courageous lies.

TRANSLATING SANDRO PENNA

The words will
not stay put
without some
sympathies.

When I pen them,
they break out,
impatient as
new petals.

> *And life is remembering*
> *a waking up*
> *all sad in a train*
> *at dawn.*

We come back.
Now, it's suburbed,
and this old man
mutters about:

'Here's that passer-by,
the most beautiful,'
as if he were a poem
to keep alive,

to love in his chance
form of heatedness
and forward moves
and strangest comfort.

THE CHEESE AND THE WORMS

I picture you as a woodcut:
grain and cribbed angles,
stood wandering
for sense in books
the size of millstones,
gristing intuitions.
Your left hand raised
as if it held a door ajar,

your eyes doubled by the strain
of reading in what light
a candle scares,
your mind in the visible,
your back as broad
and darkly confident
as your cosmology –
the curdled universe
with her angelic worms.

You turn the page
with the prickled care
of a bat above
untrod water in
the mouth of a cave,
where you are,
leant against
the days to come.

FEBRUARY

It is February. The prose of you
as you latch the door,

bundle supplies on the kitchen top
and leave the receipt on the side,

stretches itself into a body of work.
Bifo writes: *the production of meaning*

and of values take the form of parthenogenesis:
signs produce signs without any longer passing

through the flesh.
There is never a poem

ready
for when you

arrive
bright hail.

THE MODERNS

like Monica Vitti –
waking with one foot
in slurs, the other
as neat
as a liftboy's wrist,

or: things dad
did not teach me.
His body, which to
know you
had to know how

he'd left it:
at twenty or so,
built like an underpass.
Find one
richer way to do

politics – without you
plural, plus also:
to second nothing but
power – even
if it showed itself,

even if it
came on the streets
and was peaceful as
a mustard stain.

A word for
patria that you write

in prose, sloppily,
in sympathy
on a classmate's cast —

for stronger bones.
How to buy milk
when there is
still time.
Mostly sex, or faith.

What to do
when a word gluts
in your mouth —
big breeze
on water, like water

on a fuse.
How to coo coo
a Goya into modern
times as
a look finds rest

on the body.
The patient lights
of history shone back
for those
who will be lost

there. Where anger
comes from, what company
it keeps and medicines.
What it
can want when it

can't. How it
lies, incoheres like colour
of a foreign city
you refused
to cry in. Tenderness:

the stairwell of
an ear's grace for
music passage, how
to love
even subtraction,

tilted to the mouth
of the den
we built from scratch
and roofed
with the skins of

animals that the moderns
had left us.

THE MOVE

The whole fragment is no more
than an inch.
You scuff it with your good foot
to indicate
the reddish parts of fossil
motion snuck
in the dirty stone. After,
we go back
to yours for coffee and pills,
ushering sun
inside the tarpaulin drapes,
admiring
what's left of the view – a hard prayer
of houses
knelt on the square for a year's
rain played out
in a day. Then, illiterates
again, beating
our language down as thistles
shoot up, dry
and mouthless, we step over
your art books
arranged as friends at a picnic:
foreigners
on the edge, translating
grass to play
and back to pliant green again.
I don't say
what you have taught me, but how
the day attends
your laugh, attends and starts
to piece
what we have known together.

CRIB

In the autumn of that year when the world, for all we knew, was set to keep growing as it was then growing and our skin too growing like the last cheer of a wave to see the beach in, we go to the anatomy theatre in the centre of the old town, on the floor of a still operational library, the entire structure of which was rebuilt piece by piece in reconstruction after the war, which although apparently flawless will have left its trace (a chisel mark here, a drop of glue there, this varnished smell) on the high-vaulted wooden rooms, the kind hard to come by outside of cramped dreams or dolls houses, in which the thinking of their original use gives them the feel of a miniature which you have been dropped inside so that when you stand in it, ancient though it is, some ersatz tang ebbs out from the trees which were minced to timber and powellised to make this hulk run aground to the concern of an enormous surgeon who might at any moment prize off the ceiling to reveal the whole space as the centre of a laboratory which now has at its heart, simply as a curiosity for studious giants, the crib where their own extradimensional science was first raised out of infancy.

We stood there, happy as lab rats.
There were so many: the men as polished furniture,
               the tongues and groove of a room
               which waits for the difference
               of skin running between us
               and raw. I caught you quiver
               and I was too, more than I can number,
               a many of powerless kuivering.
               That will be winter we say,
               and joy from its high window.

PORTRAIT OF THE ARTIST SOUTINE BY HIS BEEF ÉCORCHÉ

I do not always want to see you in it – my red on blue, a red that is the blow
of your yell caught in the throat and pumped to the inner of your eardrum.
Then the brighter red, close to yellow, that floors the better half. A blue
that is not water but might boil or freeze all the same, like an alien element
that leaves off red to the flies which, burst present from their amber,
brim to attention the beef, me – *as if let down from the sky.*

You're drinking a lime tea, the only drink you are allowed. It is August.
This red hour, heat at its distance, is what remains of the friends who got away.
The streets outside are hosting soldiers who flirt. Your stomach is plagued
with ulcers. You eat slow, you work fast, and you have me even in your sweat,
in the yellow stains round the shoulders and the groin, our gives and hollows,
as you paint in the shut room and wait for the news you can't imagine.

One long retreat from day colour. A boy, you ran into the forest at dark
with two sugar lumps and a wet potato clutched in your sleeve to paint
where the senses scout ahead, batlike against the flax and eaves
of your Grand Guignol childhood. You're far from brick as an instrument
of innovative assault. There are hours until morning will lathe the jet sky
and let fall black particles which rest, pocketed, in slow waking eyes.

In the barn there is a big-bellied cow. She hears the rye rippling, sees
you have come home without sleep. The butcher in black and white
rolls up his sleeves. There is prayer with a human voice – *you for death
me for life* – and there is a joyful expression on the human face.
Your grandfather turns his stool and sighs. The song of a nuthatch
is dashed to the lip of recollection and the red pieces fall apart.

Or with bought colours to illude men's sense – first, charcoal sketches.
Thin likenesses that are taboo until the butcher beats you pink
for his father's one. I know your mother filed a complaint: twelve rubles
compensation hurries you to Minsk then Vilna, the pocked grey
of modern schools, the existences of rails, pianos, and Dreyfus,
grave silences that tell how they have not excused everything.

You paint the particle nature of light: a black iron rod and a clear glass
once heated to the same temperature will emit the same spectrum of light.
Likewise, I find you shining heat equivalent to the canvas in time,
and in another poem I am the bullhead rail that spits its red
under you in the caboose, head against the glass, warming under
summer's last government. My red is yours and it is cut, come in.

ς

Then we're closer. At local midnight, cold and queer blue. Known French:
passage de Dantzig. Still more than ever *astonished to be alive*
on the cream carpet of the city's print. You come to Paris,
dead nervous of its largess, redoubling their efforts to make you
paranoid as you go on looking after that phenomenal comfort
of coherence which meat, all told, can serve you up on a plate.

Fresh from the Vaugirard slaughterhouse, you put my legs in the air.
So strapped I am let go to grace, the claque of insects and the prick
of your distractions. You, my mudlark, carry a knife between your teeth
should the waters come too close, as you go on your nerves
which pop like damp logs burning in the rivered air of autumn.
You cut the canvas, as if to get out from inside, and then begin again.

If we met once before, it was on the train that brought you here.
I heard your voice, buckled up, pass by. You talked of how your work
was irresolvable – your love for it for that – and art as the professed
condition of the past in the present, the scab of sentiments forced
to air. You tell me that my yesterdays are yours but you cannot
take them out without injury – you could, but you would break the skin.

Thankfully, we have the abattoirs. Paulette goes out with a milk bottle
twice a day to buy back blood. They say you have painted the shudder:
the subject's last defence against depression, a prelude to psychic death,
as if I were tracks of your body, knuckling under pain and its distrust.
But the blood flows back, like mercy, and this shudder is not prelude
but sequel – the question of our colours as asked from a future.

In the meantime, you are black and white – Hervé Guibert's man,
his spathed back to the door catching sun at the window. *He was awake,*
nbsp; now he sleeps.
His head is all but gone in smoke. The light has the light of a haemorrhage
of light that takes light from the room, the room is what is left of what the body
can not want to take, the warmth in the room is what the body is of the light.

We meet again protagonist. Now you are candidly adding the blood
before it dries. There's no metaphor; only alchemy and failure.
Blood that taken as a general condition makes the past present,
if we mean by past: alive, if we mean by present: to be passed over.
I'll add that it is healthy of me to have stayed so beefy. The improbability
of this (my skin as occasion for your scream) is not in the least lost on me.

ς

Even the simplest colour has worried your cheek. The studio is stained
with its uses and spit. The slow work of histolysis moves my nouns
to gerunds – bleeding, heading and shouldering, spitting and scabbing.
I have begun to smell, the neighbours whinge. Police suggest ammonia,
spirit of hartshorn or sal volatile, injected twice daily. The gas rises
when the jar is opened. The room's exacting ambience is in spate.

My body dives down to the chemocline, where water meets with
other sorts of life. There are no men here but heads and knees
and lungs and jaws dispersed like colours on a wet palette.
There is Clara Immerwahr, crying foul. There is tender mud
that wrings what light reaches it. You can't but rescue me
with seemingness – the blue net trawled from the surface

that takes one month to come to air and when it does, is torn
across, and riveted with yellow seeds, dripping pigments,
hatched like isinglass, it has me caught, red in its mesh.
You direct your look to parts – the open chest, the headless base –
that are of most affect. No body lasts to be read,
though our eyes' first alphabet is for the human face.

That I should be then and you should be now is one instrument
shared by power and paint. So little of both depends on parts –
the blue, the yellow, and the red. You will find them together
despite their separate honesties, just as the one window
is opened, just as a joint squeals its clear note and air relieves
itself of chemicals and then the flies adjust to the humidity.

You head out alone, happy all the butcher's blows remain with me.
The street is only fast since your gathering's slowed you down
as when at sea, with red froth on top of the water's vaulted blue,
he stops to remember the parts. It is hard, as hard to remember
as a sentence left in the gut, that is bare of voice or breath,
the throat's thin translations that make this living out of life.

THETIC

> *Wherever cruelty is possible, and it almost always is, finding some way to avoid it will be more important than anything else.*
> Malcolm Bull

cruelty is possible
wherever
and is almost always it

to avoid finding it some way
more will be important,
else

DUCTS

Outwardly identical to the gerund, the present participle
has an altogether different origin. / The first is a resilient appositive.
Developing from the Old English *-ung*, / it enlivens the picture,
giving it verve, / as chords brush shape / onto air in the throat:

> *Looke sanguine at the breake of day, and turneth by and by*
> *To white at rising of the Sunne.*

The rising of the sun points through the present / to all instances
of the action / so that they seem (the sun that rises) / caught in a loop
(of rising), / a pivot between motion (it rises)

and image
(rising).

The participle is a kind of verbal run-off, often used to make a noun
move (run) / in a determined way (off), as the composition shifts / or
some action is brought to the fore. / Its attachment to the verb *be*
to form the progressive tense gets going relatively late. / Often paired
with a preposition, it lends action to a state or is latched / adjectivally
to a noun:

> *The quivering veynes without a skin lay beating nakedly.*
> *The panting bowels in his bulke ye might have numbred well,*

The skin lay beating is the skin that is beating. If it weren't beating,
it would not then be the skin that lies, now and then, before our nose.

The veins are quivering and the bowels are panting.
Only in the seventeen hundreds did the use in progressive aspects

expand rapidly across times, / mapping future routes for prospects and states of being, until: *I will / be quivering.*

The distinction between these two *-ings* often passes / unobserved. In the case of *keep*, for example, do we know if the part that follows is a nominalisation or not?

> *I keep (I go on) panting*
> *I keep (with me) panting*

For what it's worth, both can help: / when you're here I keep panting, when you're not I keep panting, / spun between the thing and the do. They are / both, after all, ducts of nature.

The rising and the beating,
the sun and the skin.

ANATOMIA

A Sardinian proverb says
that bones do not interest the devil
perhaps because skeletons give a great peace,
arranged in display cases or inside desert scenarios.
I love their smile made only of teeth, their cranium,
the perfection of the sockets, the missing nose,
the blank around the sex
and finally the hairs, these frills, flown into nothing.

It isn't a taste for the macabre,
but the stark realism of anatomy
praise of exactness and clarity.
Thinking ourselves skinless does us good.
To paradise there might be no better way
than returning stones, knowing ourselves heartless.

Translation of Antonella Anedda, 'Anatomia', *Historiae*.

FRAGMENT: BERLIN 3024

    half water, they are cut
    into manageable quivers,
    their outer rinds stripped
    back for the softer pith
    and then collected, one
    above the other, beaten,
    left to pant in the sun,
    and endlessly scoured
    with a stone tool –
    a rock, a shell or ivory

III

OCHRE PITCH
for Alessio

There is a selflessness in any past: at root,
it will not fold. Tonight, there are the pines
placed as though falling for each other
and, across the way, the neighbouring roof
snubs a sky of blues and an excitable red.
I would like to give this light a name, call it
something, learn it good. But it won't answer.
It only gives itself, beside the water pump,
which rattles on: *enough, enough, enough*

I had taken the ferry, and on the ferry, Chiara
had said: the colony. And I had said: family album,
roots, schooling, tea and jam, the white veranda
on which my uncle and his brother are burning
citronella oil to keep mosquitoes at bay, while nana
cricks a cigarette in a gloved hand, years learning
to hide inside that smoke. At 5am sharp: Tavolara,
the ochre of its cliffs pitched up towards a sky
marbled pink and pressing into wideness.

that this new tongue I have is bedded on your
kindnesses. I mean the kindness of a lemon tree
you planted three years ago in a garden without
much grammar or adequate soil but astonishingly
braved by life: green and gem yellows cowled
at this hour by the mountain that we're climbing
tomorrow. It is a tongue that can be powerless,
broken and shared out like a stack of *carasau*,
a kind of passing tribute to the land's curve south.

the day we arrive, forty years since they bombed
Bologna centrale. Don't spare me the violence
of this talk, or think that we can do it honestly
with words. We will talk it out, driving less
at the event, more at its incredibility, the long
pain of knowing why, when, how, and guessing
who's to blame. A show of guilt which wrongs
the innocent, who have no use for explanations
and would have lived without commemoration.

We walk down to Cala Luna. The scale of it all
is overturned: each stone an island, the island
one stone. Pines that syllable the old trail
with their needling, a trail that pipes in a wind
as bold and slight as the lizard's going sparkle.
Disordered words that land on sea prickled
ears, until it all sounds one rocking laughter.
You, setting out the coffee flask in a cave
above, and I catch only: *Kafka is in love.*

We're going inland to hunt for some *Nuraghe*,
in your dad's car, with a map that plots the castles
as blue huts next to picnic spots and panorama.
Your town slides off, one garage and flag at a time.
I pick out the way that the builder-giants roamed
when there were builders, we could say, if taken by
some myth-trodden dream of hurt and gloominess.
The brace of old faces in the bars that stare down
the sun clawing its way into their awninged lair.

Way out, past the careful plots and subplots
and fenced peripheries, there is a wedding scene,
a village come out to cheer on what may be love,
comedy of efforts and care. A knowing tendency,
that queer habit of doubt, pinches our wonder
just as we notice that smoke is wheeling up
there, where a forest is cut back to jolts of wood
in this valley cleared for centuries, still home
to a joy and a music that not one of us owns.

A landscape bitten to the edge of abstraction,
not loved, but prised of love, and not named,
not even traced in letters but like the seathreads
that lap and clothe this island dressing whoever
should need it. The radio brings disaster's progress.
The sky, adjusted for contaminants, shivers out
the awns and then distends its sickbay drape
around the old orange cork trees, severed
down the middle with such caesarean exactness

that the mere immediacy of sight is punctured.
There is an anger in everything. The corks
ripped from their bristled jackets, bellies nude
and pocked with climbing dew, lean to earth –
heroes stacked on their blunt swords of shade.
A neutrality collapses. You narrate the war
that put NATO on the coast. On your word,
two fighter jets rise – bulls of foam in unbearable
suspension – barrel over us, cordage strained

to break. The sky reels in its loafing clouds,
spread like cattle cut to bloodless chunks
by a madman's axe. Then a thin quiet ploughs
the roadside, ruts the very air with a sunless
calm, as the blue of Gioacchino's dream rounds
the mountain. We two peasants pause to piss
on a dry stone wall, splashing the thirsty grass,
the car crouched back, picking up its blissed
out tunes again. Then, you: look, there it is.
eccolo

There, ahead of us, down the valley, we do not
find a fortress. What I had thought would be
a towering thing was a handsome bag of stone,
a botched minaret, a sandcastle knocked down
on a prehistoric shore.　　We hop the gate
and stalk towards it as if the walls could rouse.
There is a ginnel of dark to enter in, a nostril
taking air and making sense of it. You first,
you first – your smile smarts then vanishes.

What we know in the dark is how to last,
the patience of stone and tang of bird shit
underfoot, the loss of your face sharpened
on memory, summer skin lapsing into dust.
How to last out together, even when apart,
even when, trespassers in the monster's hut,
we are of manner more than two: father,
friend, disasters, whatever is left of the light
that gets in and seams the soil so tight.

Light brittle with evening, the late sun
excludes its ends, lying rich in a hoofmark
or the bags of your eyes. The palms listen
on the stone, touch probes for guesswork,
slate and salt, whatever it is weakening
into tender muck.   Estuaries of song:

> there is a brick floating on the river,
> there is the river holding a brick,
> there is us comprehending the risk.

Why heroic? *I couldn't give a fuck.*
Your answer is always a diver's launch
      into blue, a brushstroke's urgent
parallel to blue, a sea-caught
      bob of hair, long arms bent,
that little sweep a hemistich, not
      stopping but allowing pause,
or the break, always to break,
      the gratitude that floats on blue.

The grammar that arranges our departures
tells us nothing of arrival. The drive back
we make the circumference of the drive out,
as though the centre had dispersed, black
and free into the fields of juniper sprouts,
out to a tidewrack with its plastics and weeds.

Keep on the horizon, everything pronounces,
and as you pass me on that scrap of Gramsci,
evening comes up with a bone in its mouth.

A space unconditional: a better idea
        than the few beats of tolerance
we tend to give ourselves. How to hear
        the moth last night? Errant as
a loanword, I half woke on its weakness,
        its awful breathy sand along
the walls. It was before me, then left
        us separate, and we slept.

the part artifice of morning   breath and
   rain packed in overnight   giddy up sunrise
   a movement down in the kitchen   a lesson
   on maps (how they age well suddenly)
   a lone tip of hair   a brush of fox marks
   the day set like a copper bust of night
   a woman laughs pragmatically outside
   not knowing   the future's real charm
   the kettle whining out its false alarm

    I, too, dislike most finished things, even if
the lake we circled today had a finish to it,
mirroring its banks up to a truss bridge
that trapped a scarce cloud. It's our chat
of small cares and goings on that sounds
like March, with its new fever, insistent
that the middles of camellias brave it out,
their redness coming on with the first fly
at home to take the temperature of fruit.

Each thing's a thief, and all the more for this.
Thistling out our pasts, the night before I go,
you to me on genre – the working hypothesis:
'I like the things you might be, [you] don't owe
me nothing.' Out front, in the day-old heat,
a bark shocks its little dog, a motor steals
into yellow, and we ourselves, pressed
for time, we can forget our names
        as foreign and indifferent ways.

and so no one is left alone in island sounds
that drift as an imperfect tense. Borrowing
warmth from the sea, the string of houses
blush their coral tones and watch the hollow
of a garden turning black. A spell of quiet
and then, upstairs, a tired voice announces
dinner's ready and a chair squeaks in reply.
Then night will eat the garden's lemons
whole and spit their seeds across the sky.

PARAPHRASE

The river seems to find us first. We realise, as our bodies laze around the bend, that it has been following us for some time. Although a moment ago it was as calm as our ignorance, the sudden sound of its new resistances falls now like your hand dropped on my shoulder as I stood waiting for you at the airport yesterday. The trees clear the way, or they have been cleared to make a way down to the bank. There's sky like you wouldn't believe, which perhaps accounts for why we hadn't seen what was below us, and we hadn't heard the river to begin with because you were busy telling me about something you'd read lately on displacement, about the gap between self-definition within and without. There was a violence in this, you'd repeated, and on each 'this' you'd flip your hands as if to move the day along. There is always elsewhere. Displacement is felt as that psychic threat to the here and now from the there and then. Reading this, I hear you say just before we hear the river, was a 'small comfort'. As if that were a cue, you stop to light a cigarette. 'Swim?' You wave the cigarette in answer. 'OK.' The way down is easier than the way up will be. I make a note of the last thing you've said so that when I get back you can pick it up again. How else had I imagined us here, together? What will comfort us when we have this page? I'm halfway through these thoughts and down the bank when you yell: 'I'm paraphrasing badly.' The water's cool and clear. I strip. The nuances of distance collapse beneath the noonday sun.

ACKNOWLEDGEMENTS

Acknowledgements are due to the editors of *PN Review* and *Prototype 5*, where earlier versions of 'Ochre Pitch' first appeared. Research for the collection was supported by a Research and Development Award (2019) from Arts Council England and a Transatlantic Travel Grant (2023) from the European Association of American Studies. Many of these poems were written during an international doctoral scholarship at Sapienza University of Rome and University of Silesia.

I thank my friends for their care and support. I am especially grateful to Alex, Amelia and Liv, who have read early drafts of these poems across the years.